BEST BARBECUES
EVER

NO NONSENSE COOKING GUIDE®

BEST BARBECUES EVER

IRENA CHALMERS

WITH
RICK RODGERS

LONGMEADOW PRESS

BEST BARBECUES EVER

Copyright © 1989 by Irena Chalmers

Published by Longmeadow Press, 201 High Ridge Road, Stamford, Connecticut 06904. No part of this book may be reproduced or used in any form or by any means, electronic or mechanical, including photocopying, recording, or by an information storage and retrieval system, without permission in writing from the publisher.

No Nonsense Cooking Guide is a registered trademark of Longmeadow Press

ISBN 0-681-40699-2

Printed in the United States of America

0 9 8 7 6 5 4 3 2 1

STAFF FOR NO NONSENSE COOKING GUIDES

EDITORIAL DIRECTION: Jean Atcheson

MANAGING EDITOR: Mary Goodbody

COVER DESIGN: Karen Skelton

ART DIRECTION & DESIGN: Helene Berinsky

ASSISTANT EDITOR: Maurice Goodbody

COVER PHOTOGRAPH: Matthew Klein

TYPESETTING: ComCom, Allentown, Pennsylvania

CONTENTS

ACKNOWLEDGMENTS

Grateful acknowledgment is made to the following for technical support and information:

Barbecue Industry Association; Kingsford Briquets; Weber-Stephen Product Company; Barbeque Wood Flavors; Flying W. Wood Products; W. W. Wood, Inc.; The California Raisin Advisory Board

BEST BARBECUES EVER

Barbecuing foods over glowing charcoal is one of the joys of warm-weather living. But there is no reason that the season for barbecuing should not extend into the cooler months of the year as well. Your backyard may not be the place to eat the November turkey, but there is no reason why it should not be cooked on the grill and enjoyed, in all its succulent splendor, indoors.

Winter, summer, spring or fall, the first step to barbecuing is deciding on the type of grill that best suits your needs. Essentially, grills either have covers or not, are large or small, are designed for charcoal or are fired by gas. Round kettles and covered cookers are the kind most often found in backyards for family use. With the lid off, these can be used to grill food directly over hot coals. With the lid on, they act rather like an oven and are also very satisfactory for smoking. Gas grills are the most expensive sort of grill you can buy. They come equipped with a propane tank or can be hooked up to a gas line. Ceramic briquets or lava rocks permanently installed in the grills are heated by the gas and in turn radiate heat to cook the food.

Small tabletops and hibachis are less expensive than

covered grills and are most often used for apartment balcony cooking, picnics and camping. These smaller models are not meant to cook large cuts of meat or whole chickens, nor can they be used for smoking, but they are perfectly satisfactory for grilling hamburgers, small fish steaks and chops.

We have developed the recipes in this book for charcoal cooking, not gas, although you can certainly make any of the recipes on a gas-fired grill. If you have only a small basic grill you will find that you will not be able to make some of the recipes—but there are plenty you *can* make. If your backyard is furnished with a kettle grill or covered cooker, you will be able to make everything on the following pages with no trouble.

When you build a fire with standard charcoal briquets, you can light it in one of several ways. The most familiar method is to stack the coals in a pyramid and light them, using lighter fluid, according to the manufacturer's instructions. You may also choose to use an electric starter or a chimney. Chimneys—inexpensive metal cylinders you fill with charcoal and then light by setting a match to a crumpled piece of newspaper under the coals—are becoming more and more popular because they are so easy to use and do not require lighter fluid. You can also use self-starting briquets, which never need additional lighter fluid. These should be spread in a single layer before they are lit.

However you light the fire, let the coals burn until they are ashy gray (at night, you will be able to see them glow red). When they are hot, spread them so that they emit even heat under the food. To test for temperature, hold your hand palm side down over the coals at cooking height. If you can hold it there for two seconds, the coals are hot, three seconds means they are medium-hot, four seconds, medium, and five seconds, low. If, while you are cooking, you find the fire too hot, raise the grid. If, on the other hand, it is too cool, knock some ash from the coals and push them closer together. You

When using liquid starter, let it soak into the briquets for at least 1 minute before lighting the fire.

can also control the heat by opening and closing the air vents, if any, on the grill: Open vents provide more heat, closed vents less heat.

After about 45 minutes, most fires require extra coals. For some cooking chores, it is a good idea to keep lit coals in a small hibachi, metal bucket or chimney to add to the fire as needed. If you add raw coals, put them around the edge of the fire and wait for 10 to 15 minutes for them to catch fire before combining them with the rest of the charcoal. This gives them time to release any noxious gases and to get sufficiently hot. Although you rarely need more than five pounds of coals for a fire, on cold and windy days you will need more charcoal. We also recommend that you buy good charcoal; bargain brands tend to burn "dirty."

If you decide to try smoking food in the grill (see Chapter 5), you will have to buy wood chips as well as charcoal. These are sold at most stores that stock charcoal, including hardware stores, specialty food stores and some supermarkets. The most common are mesquite, hickory, alder wood and the fruit woods (apple, cherry and peach wood are popular). For most purposes, wood chips should be soaked before being tossed on the hot fire. Their aromatic smoke provides flavor—they are not a source of fuel. Use them sparingly, one or two handfuls at a time, and try to follow our recommendations for the kinds of chips to use with various foods. Once you get used to using them, you will want to experiment with different chips and different foods.

Most kitchens are stocked with enough utensils for successful barbecuing, but if you plan to do a lot of outdoor cooking, it is advisable to buy a few accessories to make barbecuing easier and safer. Long-handled tongs, brushes and spatulas are the most important tools, and if they have wooden handles, they will not get as hot. It is a good idea to buy a set of long, wooden-handled skewers, too. Heavy, flame-resistant oven mitts are also helpful. You might want to invest in a hinged grill basket for cooking fish and chicken parts. Depending on your preferences, you will find rib racks and slow-turning rotisseries extremely useful, too.

Once you have finished barbecuing for the day, clean the cooled grid with a wire brush (easier to do if you have oiled it lightly before cooking) and dump the ashes from the grill. Some outdoor chefs line their grills with heavy-duty aluminum foil to make clean-up easy. In any case, you should wipe out the inside of the grill from time to time with a damp sponge and baking soda. The outside of the grill ought to be cleaned periodically, too.

Barbecuing is a simple and satisfying way to cook all sorts of food. Relaxing and pleasurable all year long, it opens up any number of possibilities for new and exciting ways to enjoy your favorite foods.

HOW MANY COALS?

To get a good idea of the number of coals you will need, spread the briquets out in a single layer under the area of the grid on which you will be cooking the food. This usually is about 5 pounds of charcoal, or 1 full chimney. When you will be cooking for longer than 45 to 50 minutes and so will be adding extra coals, estimate that you will need to add 6 or 7 raw or already lit coals at a time to maintain the correct temperature. For smoking food, you will need to begin with about 2 pounds of charcoal.

CHAPTER 1

BARBECUING SIMPLE MEATS

Surely more than any other kind of food, meat comes to mind when we think of backyard barbecues. "Come on over and we'll toss some burgers on the grill," is a familiar invitation all across the land during the warm summer months. It seems that even folks who do not particularly like hamburgers any other way enjoy them grilled to juicy perfection over hot charcoal. The same goes for steak and sausages, but have you considered grilling pork chops, a butterflied leg of lamb or a pork roast?

In this chapter we have recipes for making the perfect backyard hamburger as well as instructions for grilling a pork roast, making spicy ribs and tasty kebabs. These recipes are not difficult. They may require marinating before cooking and basting while they cook, but all are easily done to glorious turns over hot coals on any sort of home grill.

Perfect Picnic Hamburgers

Serves 6

Here is the best and easiest way to grill those all-American favorites—hamburgers. Homemade condiments make a real difference, too.

> *2 1/2 pounds ground beef*
> *Salt and pepper*
> *Homemade Ketchup (see page 76)*
> *Homemade Mustard (see page 77)*
> *Homemade Mayonnaise (see page 78)*
> *6 hamburger buns*

Salting meat before grilling quickly seals in juices during cooking.

Make a hot charcoal fire according to the directions on pages 8–10.

Form the ground beef into 6 firm but not compact patties, about 1 inch thick. Season both sides with salt and pepper to taste. Cook the patties on a lightly oiled grill over the hot coals for about 3 minutes. Turn and cook for 4 minutes for medium-rare burgers. For medium burgers, cook for 4 minutes on the first side, then turn and cook for about 7 minutes. For well-done burgers, cook for 4 minutes on the first side, then 10 to 12 minutes on the second side.

Serve the burgers immediately with Homemade Ketchup, Mustard and Mayonnaise on hamburger buns.

MEXICAN BURGERS
Serve the hamburgers with Guacamole and Roasted Tomato Salsa (see pages 71 and 72).

ITALIAN BURGERS
Top each hamburger with a slice of mozzarella cheese and cover during the last 2 minutes of cooking. Serve with warmed spaghetti sauce.

Grilled Sirloin Steaks with Thyme Butter

Serves 6

When the time is right for a nice big, juicy steak, consider only the best, most tender cuts of meat. Filet mignon, T-bone, porterhouse and rib eye steaks work well grilled as we describe here. Tougher, less expensive cuts such as round, chuck, flank and skirt steaks, while delicious grilled, benefit from being tenderized in a marinade first. The thyme butter is especially good with a perfectly cooked steak, although you might prefer another herb-flavored butter instead.

> *6 8-ounce sirloin steaks*
> *Salt and pepper*
> *Thyme Butter (see page 54)*

Build a hot charcoal fire according to the directions on pages 8–10. When the coals are hot, spread them along the bottom of the grill, banking one side so it has more coals than the other.

Season the steaks on both sides with salt and pepper to taste. Cook the steaks on a lightly oiled grill, directly over the hotter, banked coals for 3 minutes to sear one side of the meat. Turn and continue cooking over the cooler side of the fire for 4 minutes for rare steak. For medium steak cook for 3 minutes over the hotter coals, turn and cook for 7 minutes. For well-done steak cook for 3 minutes on the first side, then 10 to 12 minutes on the second side. Top each steak with a pat of Thyme Butter and serve immediately.

How do you tell if your steak is done just the way you like it? Touch it. A rare steak is soft, medium steak gives slightly, well-done meat is firm.

Beef Fajitas

Serves 6

Tender, slightly spicy slices of rare steak tucked in a warm tortilla and topped with salsa and guacamole make a tasty sandwich for lunch or supper. Kids love these—try them for a party of teenagers.

> *1 cup olive oil*
> *1/3 cup lime juice*
> *3 tablespoons Worcestershire sauce*
> *2 tablespoons fresh or canned chopped green chilies*
> *2 tablespoons chopped fresh oregano or 2 teaspoons dried*
> *1 1/2 teaspoons cumin*
> *2 cloves garlic, crushed*
> *1 1/2-pound round steak, about 1 inch thick*
> *12 flour tortillas*
> *Salt and pepper*
> *Roasted Tomato Salsa (see page 72)*
> *Guacamole (see page 71)*
> *1 cup sour cream*

Combine the olive oil, lime juice, Worcestershire sauce, chilies, oregano, cumin and garlic in a bowl. Marinate the round steak in the olive oil mixture for 2 hours at room temperature or for at least 4 hours and up to overnight chilled.

Make a hot charcoal fire according to the directions on pages 8–10.

Stack the tortillas and wrap them in a double thickness of aluminum foil. Heat the tortillas on the outside edge of the grill over hot coals, turning the packet often, for 15 minutes.

Remove the steak from the marinade and season to taste with salt and pepper.

On another spot on the grill, cook the steak over the hot coals, turning once, for 10 minutes total for medium-rare meat.

Unwrap the tortillas. Thinly slice the meat on the diagonal across the grain. Put a couple of slices of meat onto each tortilla and garnish with the salsa, guacamole and sour cream to taste. Roll up the tortillas and serve.

Pork Chops with Teriyaki Marinade

Serves 6

Grilled pork chops are absolutely delicious and must never be forgotten when you are thinking about outdoor cooking. These, flavored with the sweet-sour goodness of the marinade, are the best.

>   *6 8-ounce bone-in, center-cut pork chops, about*
>   *1 inch thick*
>   *Teriyaki Marinade (see page 59)*

Marinate the pork chops in the marinade in a bowl for 2 hours at room temperature or for at least 4 hours and up to overnight chilled.

Make a medium-hot charcoal fire according to the directions on pages 8–10.

Cook the pork chops on a lightly oiled grill over the medium-hot coals, covered, turning once, for 20 minutes or until the meat shows no pink when cut near the bone. Serve immediately.

Star-Spangled Barbecued Ribs

Serves 6 to 8

For the taste of Texas in your own backyard, try these spareribs, rubbed with pungent spices first and then mopped with a good red barbecue sauce during the last 20 minutes of cooking.

> *5 pounds spareribs*
> *Double recipe of Texas Dry Rub (see page 56)*
> *Star-Spangled Barbecue Sauce (see page 55)*

Rub the spareribs on both sides with the Texas Dry Rub. Wrap them tightly in aluminum foil and let them stand at room temperature for 2 hours or for at least 4 hours and up to overnight chilled.

Make a medium-hot charcoal fire according to the directions on pages 8–10.

Cook the spareribs on a lightly oiled grill over the medium-hot coals, turning often, for 45 minutes. Unwrap the ribs. Add additional hot coals and sprinkle the coals with soaked, drained hickory or mesquite wood chips, if desired. Baste the ribs on both sides with the barbecue sauce and cook, covered, for 10 minutes. Turn the ribs and cook, still covered, for another 10 minutes until the pork is tender. Cut the ribs between the bones and serve immediately.

Pork Roast Carolina Style

Serves 6

Cooking a rolled pork roast after it has been marinated in a tangy, peppery sauce recalls the excellent taste of true North Carolina barbecue—without the fuss. The wood chips add authentic flavor but are not crucial to the success of this wonderful dish.

> *3 to 3 1/2-pound rolled boneless pork roast*
> *Carolina Vinegar Baste (see page 56)*
> *Salt*

Marinate the pork roast in the Carolina Vinegar Baste in a bowl at room temperature for 2 hours or for up to 4 hours chilled.

Build a hot charcoal fire according to the directions on pages 8–10. The fire should be built on one side of the bottom of the grill. Put a heatproof pan on the other side.

When the fire is hot, remove the pork roast from the marinade and season with salt to taste. Cook the roast on a lightly oiled grill over the pan, covered, for 45 minutes, basting often with the remaining marinade. Add additional hot coals and sprinkle them with soaked, drained hickory wood chips, if desired. Cook the roast for another 45 minutes until a meat thermometer registers 155 degrees. Remove the roast from the heat and let it stand for 10 minutes.

Bring any remaining marinade to the boil in a small saucepan. Slice the roast and serve with the marinade alongside.

Covering a grill will help control flare-ups. If your grill has a damper, closing it will also reduce the flames. Squirt the coals with water from a spray bottle only in emergencies.

Butterflied Leg of Lamb

Serves 6

Yogurt and mint, mixed with plenty of garlic and lemon and a little cumin, make a marinade that brings the flavors of exotic North Africa to your home. Lamb is the perfect meat for this marinade—and a butterflied leg of lamb is one of the best meats for any grill. Because the thickness of butterflied lamb is uneven, the meat will not cook to a uniform doneness. For the best flavor, we suggest cooking it until most of the meat is medium-rare.

1 cup plain yogurt
1 small onion, finely chopped
2 cloves garlic, finely chopped
3 tablespoons chopped fresh mint or
  1 tablespoon dried
3 tablespoons lemon juice
Grated rind of 1 large lemon
1 teaspoon cumin
6-pound leg of lamb, boned and butterflied
Salt and pepper

For an extra burst of smoky flavor, toss dried or fresh herbs onto burning coals. Try rosemary with lamb or chicken, thyme with beef and basil with fish.

Combine the yogurt, onion, garlic, mint, lemon juice, lemon rind and cumin in a bowl and stir until well mixed. Marinate the lamb in the yogurt mixture at room temperature for 2 hours or for at least 4 hours or up to overnight chilled.

Build a hot charcoal fire on one side of the bottom of the grill according to the directions on pages 8–10. Put a heatproof pan on the other side.

Remove the lamb from the marinade and season to taste with salt and pepper. Cook the lamb on a lightly oiled grill over the hot coals, turning once, for 10 minutes. Cook over the pan for an additional 30 minutes for mostly medium-rare meat. Remove the lamb from the heat and let it stand for 10 minutes, then slice across the grain and serve immediately.

Marinated Lamb Shish Kebabs

Serves 6

Suspend the kebabs over a jelly roll pan or other shallow dish and brush the remaining marinade over them. This will make them easy to carry outside and once the skewers are set on the grill, you can easily brush the excess marinade collected in the bottom of the dish over the kebabs.

> *2½ pounds boneless leg of lamb, cut into 18*
> *1½-inch cubes*
> *Red Wine Marinade (see page 60)*
> *1 small onion, cut into 6 wedges*
> *6 medium-size plum tomatoes, cut into 12*
> *1-inch pieces*
> *2 medium-size zucchini, trimmed, cut into 12*
> *1-inch pieces*
> *Salt and pepper*

Marinate the lamb cubes in the Red Wine Marinade for 2 hours at room temperature or for at least 4 hours and up to overnight chilled.

Build a hot charcoal fire according to the directions on pages 8–10.

Remove the lamb from the marinade, reserving the marinade. Thread the meat and vegetables on each of 6 skewers in the following order: onion, lamb, tomato, lamb, zucchini, tomato, zucchini, lamb. Baste the meat and vegetables with the reserved marinade and season with salt and pepper to taste.

Cook the shish kebabs on a lightly oiled grill over the hot coals, turning often, for about 8 minutes for medium-rare meat. Slip the meat and vegetables off the skewers and serve immediately.

OILING THE GRILL

Use a brush or wadded paper towel to spread a thin layer of oil on a grill before cooking. Spray vegetable oils work well, too, as does a mixture of vegetable oil and lecithin in a spray bottle mixed in a ratio of two to one. Oiling the grill keeps food from sticking and makes clean-up easier. But go gently—too much oil will cause flare-ups. If there is a lot of oil in a marinade, you might consider skipping this step altogether.

CHAPTER 2

BARBECUING POULTRY

The grill is one of the best places to cook chicken and other poultry. The flavor of most poultry only improves when marinated for several hours in a full-flavored brew of oil, vinegar, lemon juice, herbs, spices, peppers and onions in varying combinations. What may well have begun in the supermarket as a mild-mannered bird achieves super-chicken status when cooked over smoldering coals, liberally and frequently basted with a gutsy sauce and tenderly tended.

Keeping the cover on the grill is a good way to insure that you will not overcook the poultry and dry it out. Making sure the coals are not too hot or, if the bird is in one large piece, that it is set over a drip pan and cooked indirectly, also helps. Cooking chicken or other poultry too quickly results in black, charred skin and dried out meat. Cooking it carefully results in tender, juicy, tasty meat that will bring a happy crowd to the table.

Ricotta and Herb-Stuffed Chicken Breasts

Serves 6

As the cheese gently melts and the chicken breasts grill to a golden turn, the flavors of the marinade mingle with those of the filling. Wonderful!

> *6 boneless chicken breasts, skin on*
> *Garlicky Lemon Marinade (see page 57)*
> *1 cup ricotta cheese*
> *2 tablespoons chopped fresh basil or*
> *   2 teaspoons dried*
> *2 tablespoons grated Parmesan cheese*
> *2 tablespoons fresh bread crumbs*
> *Salt and pepper*

Marinate the chicken breasts in the marinade in a bowl for 2 hours at room temperature or for up to 8 hours chilled.

Make a medium-hot charcoal fire according to the directions on pages 8–10.

Put the ricotta, basil, Parmesan and bread crumbs in a bowl and mix with a fork. Remove the chicken breasts from the marinade and slip your fingers between the skin and meat of one. Stuff the breast with about one-sixth of the cheese filling. Repeat with the remaining breasts. Season to taste with salt and pepper.

Cook the breasts on a lightly oiled grill over the medium-hot coals, covered, skin side up, for 4 minutes. Turn and cook, covered, for about 4 minutes. Let the chicken breasts stand for a couple of minutes, then slice diagonally. Serve the chicken breasts hot, warm or at room temperature.

Whole Roast Chicken with Rosemary and Lemon

Serves 4

This has to be one of the easiest and most foolproof ways to barbecue chicken. Set the bird on the grill and forget about it. The herb mixture sprinkled in the cavity before cooking lends subtle flavor to the roast meat—and the olive oil rubbed over the chicken makes the skin especially crispy.

4-pound whole chicken
Salt and pepper
3 tablespoons chopped fresh rosemary or
*   1 tablespoon dried*
1 large lemon, quartered
3 cloves garlic, crushed
Olive oil

Make a hot charcoal fire according to the directions on pages 8–10. The fire should be on one side of the bottom of the grill. Put a heatproof pan on the other side.

Wash the chicken inside and out under cold running water and pat it dry with paper towels. Sprinkle the cavity lightly with salt and pepper. Stuff the cavity with rosemary, lemon and garlic and skewer the tail vent shut with toothpicks. Truss the chicken with cotton twine. Rub it with olive oil and season to taste with salt and pepper.

When the fire is hot, cook the chicken on a lightly oiled grill over the pan, covered, basting often with olive oil, for about 2 hours until a meat thermometer inserted in the fleshy part of the thigh registers 165 to 170 degrees. Let the chicken stand for 10 minutes before carving. Serve the chicken hot, warm or at room temperature.

Large pieces of meat and whole chickens cook best with indirect heat. This means that the coals are set on one side of the grill and a drip pan on the other. The bird is placed over the pan, which catches its drippings.

Chicken Halves Dijon

Serves 8

While the chicken cooks briskly over glowing coals, use a long-handled brush to slather the sharp, piquant mustard sauce generously over the meat. Cooking chickens halved, rather than whole or cut into small sections, leaves them nice and juicy yet easy to manage over a hot grill.

> 1 cup Dijon mustard
> 1/4 cup white wine
> 1/4 cup olive oil
> 2 scallions, trimmed and chopped
> 2 tablespoons chopped fresh tarragon or
>   2 teaspoons dried
> 1/8 teaspoon Tabasco sauce
> 2 3 1/2-pound chickens, halved
> Salt and pepper

Make a medium-hot charcoal fire according to the directions on pages 8–10.

Put the mustard, white wine, olive oil, scallions, tarragon and Tabasco sauce in a bowl and mix well. Season the chicken on both sides with salt and pepper to taste.

Cook the chicken on a lightly oiled grill over the medium-hot coals for 10 minutes, turning once. Continue cooking, covered, turning and basting frequently with the mustard mixture, for 30 minutes or until the juices run clear yellow when the chicken is pierced. Serve hot, warm or at room temperature.

Ginger Chicken

Serves 4 to 6

These chicken pieces marinate for a short time in a gingery, sweet-sour marinade before being barbecued in less than 30 minutes over smoldering coals.

> *1/2 cup soy sauce*
> *1/4 cup sherry*
> *2 tablespoons lemon juice*
> *1 teaspoon sugar*
> *1/4 teaspoon cayenne pepper*
> *1 clove garlic*
> *1-inch piece fresh ginger, peeled and finely chopped*
> *3 1/2- to 4-pound chicken, cut into pieces*

Combine all the ingredients except the chicken in a saucepan and bring to the boil. Remove from the heat and let the marinade cool to lukewarm.

Put the chicken pieces in a bowl and pour the marinade over them. Marinate for 30 minutes at room temperature or for up to 4 hours chilled. Turn the chicken pieces several times to insure that they are evenly coated.

Build a medium-hot charcoal fire following the directions on pages 8–10.

Drain and dry the chicken, reserving the marinade. Cook over the medium-hot coals, skin side down, basting frequently with the marinade, for 7 to 8 minutes for white meat, 15 to 16 minutes for dark meat. Turn the chicken pieces over and continue cooking for the same amounts of time until the chicken is done and nicely glazed. Serve hot, warm or at room temperature.

Poultry and meat should be at room temperature before they are barbecued. We suggest marinating food at room temperature, but if your schedule dictates that you leave the food in the refrigerator while marinating, take it out about 30 minutes before grilling to allow it to warm up.

Cornish Game Hens with Orange Glaze

Serves 4

Plump little game hens are ideal for grilling. With a slightly gingery orange-flavored marinade and baste, they take on a rich taste enhanced by the distinctive aroma of the burning charcoal.

1 1/2 cup orange juice
3/4 cup vegetable oil
1/4 cup soy sauce
1/4 cup lemon juice
2 tablespoons chopped fresh ginger
2 cloves garlic, chopped
2 Cornish game hens, split down the backbone
Salt and pepper
1 cup orange marmalade
3 tablespoons Dijon mustard

Put the orange juice, oil, soy sauce, lemon juice, ginger and garlic in a bowl and mix well. Marinate the game hens in this mixture for 2 hours at room temperature or for up to 8 hours chilled.

Make a medium-hot charcoal fire according to the directions on pages 8–10.

Remove the hens from the marinade and season to taste with salt and pepper. Reserve the marinade.

Put the marmalade and mustard in a bowl with 4 tablespoons of the reserved marinade and mix well.

Cook the hens on a lightly oiled grill over the medium-hot coals, covered, turning once, for 20 minutes. Cook, covered, turning and basting often with the marmalade mixture, for another 40 minutes until the juices run clear when the meat is pierced with a knife. Serve the game hens hot, warm or at room temperature.

Roast Roulade of Turkey

Serves 6 to 8

Here, a flattened breast is rolled around a simple ham and cheese filling and grilled to juicy perfection over hot coals.

> *4-pound turkey breast, boned, skin on*
> *10–12 fresh basil leaves or 10 fresh spinach*
> *leaves, washed and stemmed, with 2 teaspoons*
> *dried basil*
> *1/4 pound Swiss cheese, thinly sliced*
> *1/4 pound boneless ham, thinly sliced*
> *Olive oil*
> *Salt and pepper*
> *1 1/2 cups white wine*

Make a hot charcoal fire on one side of the grill according to the directions on pages 8–10. Put a heat-proof pan on the other side.

Lay the turkey breast, skin side down, on a work surface and pound with a mallet to flatten slightly. Arrange the basil leaves over the surface of the meat. (If you are using spinach leaves, sprinkle the dried basil over the spinach leaves.) Arrange the cheese over the basil, and the ham over the cheese. Starting at the long side of the breast, roll it up tightly. Tie the breast at 2-inch intervals with cotton twine, rub it with olive oil and season with salt and pepper to taste.

When the fire is hot, pour 1 cup of white wine into the pan in the grill. Cook the turkey breast, covered, over the pan, basting often with the remaining 1/2 cup of wine, for about 2 hours until a meat thermometer registers 155 degrees. Let the turkey breast stand for 10 minutes before slicing. Serve it hot, warm or at room temperature.

Turkey breasts are fast becoming a favorite way to eat turkey. Not as large as a whole turkey—which is a boon for small families—they take less time to cook.

CHAPTER 3

BARBECUING FISH AND SEAFOOD

Fish is quickly gaining in popularity as a favorite for backyard barbecuing. It is low in fat, high in nutrition, cooks quickly and tastes absolutely wonderful. What could be better?

Fish and shellfish often benefit from gentle marinating, picking up the subtle flavors of herbs and mild spices. Because fish is so delicate, you must be careful not to leave it in the marinade for too long or it will begin to "cook" and lose both taste and texture when you come to grill it. Most fish does not need to be turned during cooking but should be watched closely— take it from the grill the moment before it begins to flake.

Guidelines to keep in mind about grilling fish are to treat it carefully, to flavor marinades and sauces with delicacy and to avoid overmarinating and overcooking. And, as with all fish cookery, it is important to begin with good, fresh fish purchased from a reliable source.

Grilled Lobster Halves

Serves 4

Grilled lobster, drenched with butter and garnished with parsley and wedges of lemon, is an impressive feast. All you need to complete it is a good white wine and fresh homemade coleslaw. For more good taste, try laying pats of Tarragon Butter (page 54) directly on the lobsters during the last three minutes of cooking. We devised this recipe for four people, as it can be tricky to fit more than four lobsters at one time on most grills.

4 1¼- to 1½-pound lobsters
8 tablespoons (4 ounces) butter, melted
Salt and pepper
Chopped parsley
Lemon wedges

Make a medium-hot charcoal fire according to the directions on pages 8–10.

Cut the lobsters at the crease behind the head—do not cut them completely through. Split the lobsters in half lengthwise. Remove the dark matter in the heads, and discard the intestinal tube that runs the length of each one. Reserve any green tomalley or red roe you might find and stir these into the melted butter. Crack the lobster claws. Season the lobsters with salt and pepper to taste and brush them with some of the melted butter.

Cook the lobsters on a lightly oiled grill over the medium-hot coals, cut sides down, for 3 minutes. Turn, brush again with butter and cook for about 4 minutes until the shells are deep red. Sprinkle the lobsters with parsley and serve immediately with lemon wedges.

Grilled Shellfish
with Salsa Verde

Serves 6

Here is a recipe that is so easy you will make it time and
again. It is as good an hors d'oeuvre as it is a summer
supper, particularly in the regions of the country where
the shellfish is as fresh as can be. Discard any clams or
mussels that do not open after five minutes or so of
grilling.

> *1 cup packed parsley leaves*
> *1/2 cup blanched slivered almonds*
> *3 tablespoons chopped fresh basil or*
>   *1 tablespoon dried*
> *1 tablespoon Dijon mustard*
> *1 tablespoon lemon juice*
> *2 cloves garlic, crushed*
> *1 cup olive oil*
> *Salt and pepper*
> *4 dozen medium oysters, scrubbed*
> *4 dozen medium littleneck clams, scrubbed*
> *Lemon wedges*

Make a hot charcoal fire according to the directions
on pages 8–10.

Put the parsley, almonds, basil, mustard, lemon juice,
garlic and olive oil in a blender or food processor and
process until smooth. Season the salsa verde with salt
and pepper to taste.

Cook the oysters and clams over the hot coals, con-
cave sides of the shells down, for 3 to 5 minutes until
the shells begin to open. Transfer the shellfish with
tongs to platters and serve immediately with the salsa
verde and lemon wedges.

Spicy Shrimp on Summer Pasta

Serves 6

With but a minute or two of forethought to mix up the tomato sauce, here is a meal you can put together at the last minute. The grill need only be fired up long enough to cook the skewered shrimp and the pasta cooks quickly on top of the stove. Just before serving, top the hot pasta with the uncooked tomato and basil sauce and hot, spicy grilled shrimp.

SAUCE:
1 pound ripe tomatoes, cored and chopped
3 tablespoons chopped fresh basil
1 clove garlic, chopped
Salt and pepper

12 ounces dark beer
1/3 cup lime juice
1/4 cup olive oil
1 small red onion, finely chopped
2 cloves garlic, chopped
1 fresh green chili, chopped
1 teaspoon chili powder
1 teaspoon paprika
36 medium shrimp, peeled and deveined, tails left on
1 pound fettuccine, cooked

A recent survey shows that when Americans entertain, they fire up the grill more than ever before. In fact, we are more likely to host a cookout than to give a formal dinner party, cocktail party or brunch. And fish is one of the best choices for entertaining at home.

Combine the chopped tomatoes, basil and garlic in a bowl and season to taste with salt and pepper. Let the sauce stand at room temperature for at least 1 hour or for up to 4 hours. Do not chill.

Combine the beer, lime juice, olive oil, onion, garlic, chili, chili powder and paprika in a bowl until well mixed. Add the shrimp and marinate at room temperature for up to 1 hour.

Make a medium-hot charcoal fire according to the directions on pages 8–10.

Remove the shrimp from the marinade. Skewer the shrimp and season to taste with salt and pepper. Cook them on a lightly oiled grill over medium-hot coals for 3 minutes, turning once, until the shrimp just turn pink. Divide the cooked fettuccine among 6 plates and spoon the tomato sauce over each portion. Top each with 6 shrimp and serve immediately.

Salmon Steaks with Roasted Tomato Salsa

Serves 6

Grilled salmon is hard to beat. After it marinates in zesty salsa for a while, it tastes even better.

> 6 6- to 7-ounce salmon steaks, about ¾ inch thick
> Roasted Tomato Salsa (see page 72)

Marinate the salmon steaks in the salsa in a bowl for 1 hour at room temperature or for up to 2 hours chilled. Do not overmarinate.

Make a medium-hot charcoal fire according to the directions on pages 8–10.

Remove the salmon steaks from the salsa and reserve the salsa. Cook the steaks on a lightly oiled grill over the medium-hot coals for about 6 minutes, turning once, until the fish just flakes with a fork. Serve immediately with additional salsa on the side.

Swordfish with Fennel

Serves 6

Fennel adds a tantalizing flavor to grilled swordfish—
and the fire smells delicious as it cooks.

6 7-ounce swordfish steaks, about 1 inch thick
Provençale Marinade (see page 58)
Salt and pepper
3 tablespoons dried fennel seeds or stems, soaked
    briefly in water and drained

Fennel seeds work
nearly as well as
the stems. If you
soak and drain
them, they will
make an aromatic
smoke and will
not burn.

Marinate the swordfish in the marinade in a bowl for
up to 2 hours at room temperature or up to 4 hours
chilled. Do not overmarinate.

Make a hot charcoal fire according to the directions
on pages 8–10.

Remove the swordfish from the marinade and season
with salt and pepper to taste.

Toss the drained fennel seeds or stems onto the hot
coals. Cook the swordfish on a lightly oiled grill over
the hot coals for about 6 minutes, turning once, until
the fish is just opaque when sliced in the center. Do not
overcook or the swordfish will dry out. Serve immediately.

DRIED FENNEL STEMS

Dried fennel stems are appearing in specialty markets with
increasing frequency. If you have not yet figured out a way to
use them, try soaking the stems briefly in water (for about 5 or
10 minutes at most), draining them and then tossing the stems
directly on hot coals.

Grilled Tuna Salad Niçoise

Serves 6

Grilled salads are truly wonderful—all the good flavor of the grill with the color and gaiety of a well-constructed salad. This one is a delicious play on a classic Niçoise, which usually includes canned tuna and black olives and always is garnished with tomatoes.

> *1 cup olive oil*
> *¼ cup lemon juice*
> *3 tablespoons chopped fresh basil or*
> *   1 tablespoon dried*
> *½ teaspoon pepper*
> *2 8-ounce tuna steaks, about 1 inch thick*
> *1 pound small new potatoes, cut into ¼-inch*
> *   slices*
> *1 pound asparagus, trimmed, cut diagonally into*
> *   1-inch pieces*
> *2 medium-size ripe tomatoes, cut into sixths*
> *1 yellow sweet pepper, seeded, ribbed and cut*
> *   into ½-inch strips*
> *1 bunch arugula or watercress, stemmed*
> *Salt and pepper*

Put the olive oil, lemon juice, basil and pepper in a bowl and mix well. Marinate the tuna steaks in the olive oil mixture at room temperature for 2 hours or for up to 3 hours chilled.

Make a hot charcoal fire according to the directions on pages 8–10.

Cook the potatoes in boiling salted water for 5 minutes until crisp-tender. Do not overcook. Using a slotted spoon, transfer the potato slices to a colander, rinse under cold running water and drain. Pat the slices dry with paper towels. In the same water, cook the asparagus for 2 minutes until crisp-tender. Drain, rinse under cold running water and drain again.

Remove the tuna from the marinade. Toss the potato slices in the marinade. Put the potato slices, slightly overlapping, if necessary, in a hinged grill basket, reserving the marinade. Cook the potato slices over the hot coals for 10 to 12 minutes, turning once, until the potatoes are golden brown. Put the cooked potatoes in a large bowl.

On another part of the grill, cook the tuna over the hot coals, turning once, for about 6 minutes. Do not overcook the tuna or it will dry out. Slice the tuna into strips and put them in a bowl. Add the tomatoes, yellow pepper, arugula, asparagus and reserved marinade. Toss, season to taste with salt and pepper and serve immediately.

CHAPTER 4

GRILLING VEGETABLES

G rilled vegetables, considered something of a novelty a few decades back, are fast becoming a well-established part of the backyard cook's repertoire. Familiar standby side dishes such as tossed green salad, potato salad and coleslaw are giving way to grilled tomatoes, vegetable kebabs and charcoal-roasted potatoes. Vegetables cooked in the open air with fresh herbs, olive oil and other seasonings taste just right with barbecued chicken, charred steak and grilled fish—so good, in fact, that many cooks find it hard to plan supper on the deck or patio without including grilled vegetables on the menu.

Most vegetables do best when set directly on a lightly oiled grill. Some grill chefs like to wrap them in foil and nestle them in the coals, but we have found that they tend to burn when cooked this way and suggest you follow our instructions for grid cooking. Watch the vegetables carefully—because they are so naturally watery, they cook quickly, and if you are not diligent, they can shrivel up before your eyes. Yet this very tendency is one of the joys of grilled vegetables; they take only minutes and they taste so awfully good.

Herbed Tomato Halves

Serves 6

These tomatoes are so easy and so fast you will want to make them every time you light the coals. And why not? Although the recipe works best with August's vine-ripened crop, it is also a good way to prepare decent hothouse tomatoes.

> *3 medium-size tomatoes, halved*
> *6 tablespoons Oregano Butter (see page 54)*
> *Salt and pepper*

Make a medium-hot charcoal fire according to the directions on pages 8–10.

Squeeze the tomato halves gently, upside down, to remove excess juice and seeds.

Grill the tomatoes, cut sides down, over the medium-hot coals for 2 minutes. Turn the tomatoes over and place 1 tablespoon of Oregano Butter on top of each half. Grill for an additional 2 minutes. Season with salt and pepper to taste. Serve hot or at room temperature.

Vegetable Kebabs

Makes 6 kebabs

Here are some traditional kebabs without the traditional marinated red meat. The oil is heated with the rosemary and then left to sit for an hour so that the full flavor of the herb is released and infused into the oil.

Wooden skewers, available at supermarkets and cookware stores, are a boon to the griller. Soak the skewers in cold water for 30 minutes and drain—unsoaked skewers will burn over hot coals.

1/2 cup olive oil
3 tablespoons chopped fresh thyme or
*   1 tablespoon dried*
1 medium-size green or red bell pepper, seeded
12 large mushrooms
2 small zucchini, scrubbed and trimmed
12 cherry tomatoes
Salt and pepper

Make a medium-hot charcoal fire according to the directions on pages 8–10.

Heat the olive oil and the thyme in a small saucepan over low heat for 3 minutes, just until the oil is warm. Set aside for at least 1 hour.

Cut the pepper into 12 1-by-1½-inch pieces. Stem the mushrooms and cut each zucchini crosswise into 6 thick pieces.

Put the vegetables onto each of 6 skewers in the following order: 1 piece of pepper, 1 cherry tomato, 1 mushroom cap, 1 piece of zucchini, 1 mushroom cap, 1 piece of zucchini, 1 cherry tomato and 1 piece of pepper. (The firmer vegetables will hold the tomatoes in place during grilling.)

Brush the kebabs well with the rosemary oil and season them to taste with salt and pepper. Grill over the medium-hot coals for 10 to 12 minutes, turning often, until the vegetables are crisp-tender. Serve hot or at room temperature.

Golden Grilled Potatoes

Serves 6

Once you begin cooking potatoes over hot coals, you will have a hard time returning to more conventional means. These turn golden and crunchy, just as they might in a frying pan, only better! Turning them as they cook is a breeze with the help of a hinged grill basket.

> *⅓ cup olive oil*
> *3 tablespoons chopped fresh rosemary or*
> *   1 tablespoon dried*
> *2 cloves garlic, crushed*
> *2 pounds medium-size new potatoes, cut into*
> *   ¼-inch slices*
> *Salt and pepper*

Heat the olive oil with the rosemary and garlic over low heat for about 3 minutes, just until the oil is warm. Remove from the heat and set aside for at least 1 hour.

Make a medium-hot charcoal fire according to the directions on pages 8–10.

Cook the potatoes in boiling salted water over high heat for about 5 minutes until crisp-tender. Do not overcook. Drain the potatoes in a colander, rinse with cold water and drain again. Pat the potato slices dry with paper towels. Put the partially cooked potato slices in a large bowl, pour the rosemary oil over the slices and toss.

Put the slices, slightly overlapping, if need be, in a hinged grill basket. Grill over the medium-hot coals for 10 to 12 minutes, turning often, until the potatoes are golden brown. Season to taste with salt and pepper and serve immediately.

Herb- or garlic-infused olive oil will keep for a month or so in the refrigerator. Make it in quantity and use often to give extra flavor to salads, marinades and pasta dishes.

Grilled Corn on the Cob with Sage Butter

Serves 6

Few summertime foods equal the exquisite flavor of freshly picked sweet corn. Buy it fresh from a local farmstand if you possibly can and cook it on the same day it is picked. Or, better yet, pick it yourself to insure freshness. If you have never tried grilled corn on the cob before, you are in for a treat—especially when it is spread with Sage Butter. We grill it on a grill rather than directly on the coals because of its tendency to burn. One ear apiece will not content most people so consider buying a few more than suggested.

> *6 medium-size ears sweet corn, husked*
> *6 tablespoons (3 ounces) Sage Butter, softened*
> *(see page 54)*
> *Salt and pepper*

Make a hot charcoal fire according to the directions on pages 8–10.

Rub each ear of corn with 1 tablespoon of the butter and wrap each in aluminum foil.

Cook the corn on the grill over the outside edge of the hot coals, turning often, for about 15 minutes until the corn is tender. Unwrap, season with salt and pepper to taste and serve immediately.

Roasted Red and Yellow Peppers

Serves 6

You can roast peppers over the gas flame of your stove or in the broiler, but they will never taste as good as when they are roasted over a hot charcoal fire. Red peppers are the classic selection for roasting—yellow, orange and purple peppers work well, too, if you can find them. Green peppers turn bitter when roasted.

> *3 medium-size sweet red peppers*
> *3 medium-size sweet yellow peppers*
> *Salt and pepper*

Make a medium-hot charcoal fire according to the directions on pages 8–10.

Core the peppers, scrape off the seeds and cut them lengthwise into quarters.

Grill, skin side down, over the medium-hot coals for about 5 minutes until the skin begins to char and blacken. Season with salt and pepper to taste and serve hot or at room temperature.

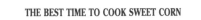

THE BEST TIME TO COOK SWEET CORN

Sweet corn should be eaten soon after picking, because the sugar in the corn begins to turn to starch as soon as the ear is detached from the plant. Some purists feel the only way to get the *true* flavor of sweet corn is to pick it yourself and then dash to the house (have the grill hot!) at breakneck speed. You may not have to be an Olympic sprinter to get the most from an ear of corn, but cooking it the same day it is picked does make a real difference in the flavor.

Roasted Red Onions

Serves 6

It is hard to find a sweeter, more tender onion dish. And it is so easy. Wrap the onions well ahead of time, if you want, and toss them directly on the coals 20 minutes before it will be time to eat. Large yellow onions work well, too. Yellow or red, these onions taste just great with grilled meat or poultry.

> *2 tablespoons (1 ounce) butter, softened*
> *6 medium-size red onions*
> *Salt and pepper*
> *2 tablespoons balsamic or red wine vinegar*

Make a medium-hot charcoal fire according to the directions on pages 8–10.

Butter one side of each of 6 12-by-9-inch aluminum foil pieces with 1 teaspoon of butter. Peel the onions and slice each one crosswise into ¼-inch-thick rings, keeping the slices in order as you go. Reform the slices of each onion back into its original round shape and put one on each of the buttered foil pieces. Don't worry if the onions are not perfectly shaped. Season with salt and pepper to taste and wrap each onion up tightly in its foil.

Cook the wrapped onions directly on medium-hot coals, turning often, for 20 to 30 minutes until tender. Unwrap, sprinkle each onion with 1 teaspoon of vinegar and serve hot or at room temperature.

Charcoal-Grilled Summer Vegetables

Serves 6 to 8

A fired-up grill spread with a colorful array of roasting vegetables is a pretty and appetizing sight. Spreading the vegetables with herbed garlic butter keeps them moist as they cook and adds wonderful flavor.

4 small potatoes
2 small eggplant
2 zucchini
2 summer squash
4 red peppers
4 tablespoons (2 ounces) butter, softened
1 tablespoon fresh basil or 1 teaspoon dried
1 tablespoon fresh thyme or 1 teaspoon dried
1 clove garlic, finely chopped
Salt
⅓ cup grated Parmesan cheese

Make a medium-hot charcoal fire according to the directions on pages 8–10.

Cut all the vegetables in half lengthwise. Core the peppers and scrape off the seeds. Combine the butter with the herbs, garlic and salt to taste. Spread the butter all over the vegetables.

Arrange the vegetables over the medium-hot coals with the potatoes in the center where the heat is strongest. Cook for 10 minutes, turn over and sprinkle with cheese. Cook for 10 minutes more or until all the vegetables are tender. If some seem done before the others, lift them from the grill and keep them on a warm platter.

For a delicious salad, let the peppers from any of these recipes cool and then toss them with herb-flavored olive oil.

SMOKING ON THE GRILL

If you have never tried smoking meat or fish on the grill, do not wait for another week to go by before doing so. The complex, woodsy flavor of food cooked over smoldering coals and smoking wood chips is hard to match. The distinctive taste of smoked foods cannot be achieved by grilling alone; it comes only from being cooked for a long period of time in a hot cloud of aromatic smoke.

If you plan to do a lot of smoking you might consider buying a water smoker—a special apparatus designed expressly for smoking. But if you are going to smoke only occasionally, a grill with a lid does a very good job. Kettle grills are preferred for home smoking; we used one for the recipes in this chapter, with splendid results. Easy as it is, smoking does take both time and diligence. You must watch the coals to be sure the correct temperature is maintained, and when need be, add more coals. It is a good idea to have extra briquets burning in an auxiliary grill, hibachi or charcoal chimney. Be sure to soak the wood chips, which produce the smoke, for at least 30 minutes and keep the bucket holding them near the grill so that you can toss some on every so often.

Once you have smoked a salmon or turkey breast, you will surely be so intrigued and excited by the taste and texture of the food that you will want to try other foods. You are in luck! The recipes here are smashing.

Smoked Salmon Steaks with Tarragon Sauce

Serves 6

This mustard sauce is derived from a Scandinavian classic often made to accompany gravlax. Smoked salmon, truly remarkable in flavor and texture, ranks as one of the best smoked dishes ever. Smoked at home, it is far more subtle and less salty than commercially smoked salmon. But it does not keep for as long, which rarely matters, as it is unlikely to last for any length of time in most households.

Remember that home smoking is for flavor only. It does not preserve the food.

> *4 tablespoons Dijon mustard*
> *3 tablespoons sugar*
> *2 tablespoons white, tarragon or white wine*
>   *vinegar*
> *1/3 cup vegetable oil*
> *3 tablespoons chopped fresh tarragon or*
>   *1 tablespoon dried*
> *6 cups water*
> *3/4 cup coarse salt*
> *3 tablespoons sugar*
> *1 teaspoon peppercorns, crushed*
> *6 6-ounce salmon steaks*

(continued)

Put the mustard, sugar and vinegar in a food processor or blender. With the machine running, slowly add the oil until the sauce is smooth. Stir in the tarragon. Let the sauce stand at room temperature until ready to serve the salmon.

Combine the water, salt, sugar and peppercorns in a bowl and stir to dissolve the salt and sugar. Put the salmon steaks in the brine, cover and chill for 2 hours. Drain the salmon, rinse well under cold running water and drain again. Put the salmon on a wire rack and air-dry for about 90 minutes until the surface of the fish is dry and shiny.

Soak a handful of wood chips in water to cover. Alder wood or apple wood are recommended for salmon.

Build a small fire (about 12 briquets) on the bottom of one side of the grill. Put a heatproof pan on the other side. When the interior of the covered grill reaches 160 degrees, drain the wood chips and sprinkle them on the hot coals. Smoke the salmon steaks on a lightly oiled grill for about 2 hours until the fish flakes, adding more hot coals and wood chips to maintain a temperature of 150 to 170 degrees. Serve the salmon hot, warm or chilled with the sauce.

If a recipe calls for air-drying, you can cut the time it takes in half by training an electric fan on the food as it dries. Air-drying seals in moisture and juices.

Smoked Bluefish with Lemon-Dill Sauce

Serves 6 to 8

Rich, tender, moist and flaky, bluefish takes to smoking better than most fish. Serve this as an appetizer with a refreshing lemon-dill sauce.

2 cups sour cream
Grated rind of 1 lemon
2 tablespoons lemon juice
2 tablespoons chopped fresh dill or
   2 teaspoons dried
2 tablespoons drained capers, chopped if large
   (optional)
1 tablespoon coarse salt
2 teaspoons sugar
$1/2$ teaspoon powdered ginger
$1/4$ teaspoon pepper
3 8-ounce bluefish fillets, skin on

Combine the sour cream, lemon rind, lemon juice, dill and capers until well mixed. Chill the sauce until ready to serve the bluefish.

Combine the salt, sugar, ginger and pepper until well mixed. Rub the mixture on both sides of the bluefish fillets. Cover and chill for 2 hours. Rinse the bluefish well under cold running water. Put the fillets on a wire rack and air-dry at room temperature for about 90 minutes until the fillets are dry and shiny.

Soak a handful of wood chips in water to cover. Alder wood is the best choice for the fish, apple wood the second best choice.

Build a small fire (about 12 briquets) on one side of the bottom of a grill. Put a heatproof pan on the other side. When the interior of the covered grill reaches 170 degrees, drain the wood chips and sprinkle them over the coals.

Smoke the fillets on a lightly oiled grill over the pan for about 2 hours until the fish flakes, adding additional hot coals and wood chips as necessary to maintain a temperature of 160 to 180 degrees. Divide the bluefish into 6 portions and serve hot, warm or chilled with the sauce.

Smoky Barbecue Shrimp

Serves 6

With the tang of barbecue sauce smoked into them, these subtle-tasting shrimp are unlike any you have tried before—sensational as an appetizer. As with all smoked food, the shrimp take time but otherwise could not be easier to prepare.

> *2 cups water*
> *2 tablespoons coarse salt*
> *2 teaspoons sugar*
> *1 teaspoon peppercorns, crushed*
> *2 pounds medium shrimp, peeled and deveined*
> *Star-Spangled Barbecue Sauce (see page 55)*

Fish and seafood are often put in brine before smoking to kill bacteria. This is not usually necessary for meat.

Combine the water, salt, sugar and peppercorns in a bowl and stir to dissolve the salt and sugar. Add the shrimp, cover and chill for 2 hours.

Drain the shrimp in a colander, rinse well with cold water and drain again. Lay the shrimp on a rack and air-dry at room temperature for about 1 hour until the surface of the shrimp is dry and shiny.

Soak a handful of wood chips in water to cover. Alder wood or mesquite are preferred for the shrimp.

Build a small fire (about 12 briquets) on one side of the bottom of a grill. Put a heatproof pan on the other side. When the interior of the covered grill reaches 160 degrees, drain the wood chips and sprinkle them over the coals.

Dip the shrimp in the barbecue sauce and thread on 6 skewers. Smoke the shrimp on a lightly oiled grill over the pan for about 90 minutes, adding more hot coals and wood chips as necessary to maintain a temperature of 150 to 170 degrees. Serve the shrimp hot, warm or at room temperature.

Smoked Pork Chops with Mango Relish

Serves 6

Now you're smokin'! The pungent mixture of spices and brown sugar mingles with the smoke from the hickory chips to produce the best-tasting pork chops you will ever put fork and knife to.

> *½ cup brown sugar*
> *2 tablespoons paprika*
> *2 teaspoons pepper*
> *1 teaspoon cayenne pepper*
> *1 teaspoon salt*
> *6 center-cut pork chops, about 1 inch thick*
> *1 cup pineapple juice*
> *¼ cup bourbon*
> *Mango Relish (see page 74)*

Combine the brown sugar, paprika, pepper, cayenne and salt. Rub the mixture onto both sides of the pork chops and let stand at room temperature for 2 hours or for at least 4 hours to overnight chilled.

Soak a couple of handfuls of wood chips in water to cover. Hickory chips are best with pork.

Build a medium fire (about 16 briquets) on the bottom of one side of the grill. Put a heatproof pan on the other side. Pour the pineapple juice and bourbon into the pan. When the interior of the covered grill reaches 200 degrees, drain the chips and sprinkle them over the hot coals.

Smoke the pork chops on a lightly oiled grill over the pan for about 2½ hours until a meat thermometer registers 160 degrees, adding additional hot coals and wood chips to maintain a grill temperature of 190 to 210 degrees. Serve immediately with Mango Relish.

1 or 2 handfuls of wood chips is sufficient for most smoking needs. Let them soak for at least 30 minutes before draining them—a quick shake ought to do it—and then sprinkle them over the coals. Chips soaked for less than 30 minutes will burn rather than smoke.

Herbed Smoked Turkey Breast with Cranberry Chutney

Serves 6 to 8

Never mind that the winds of November may blow chill—try smoking a turkey breast next Thanksgiving, and you may be setting a trend for the years that follow. The white meat of the turkey breast gently absorbs the smoke to produce moist, full-flavored meat that, once at the table, is deliciously offset by a bold cranberry chutney.

> *12-ounce bag fresh or frozen, defrosted*
>   *cranberries*
> *3/4 cup cider vinegar*
> *2/3 cup packed brown sugar*
> *1 small onion, chopped*
> *1 tablespoon chopped fresh ginger*
> *1 fresh or canned green chili, chopped*
> *1 clove garlic, chopped*
> *1 cinnamon stick*
> *8 tablespoons (4 ounces) butter, softened*
> *1 tablespoon chopped parsley*
> *1 tablespoon chopped fresh sage or*
>   *1 teaspoon dried*
> *1 tablespoon chopped fresh rosemary or*
>   *1 teaspoon dried*
> *1 tablespoon chopped fresh thyme or*
>   *1 teaspoon dried*
> *1 tablespoon chopped shallots or scallions*
> *Salt and pepper*
> *4-pound turkey breast, boned, skin on*
> *1 cup dry white wine*

Put the cranberries, vinegar, brown sugar, onion, ginger, chili, garlic and cinnamon stick in a saucepan over moderate heat. Cook gently for 30 minutes, remove the cinnamon stick and cool. Chill the chutney until you are ready to serve the turkey breast.

Soak a couple of handfuls of wood chips in water to cover. Hickory, apple or mesquite is preferred.

Build a small fire (about 12 briquets) on the bottom of one side of the grill. Put a heatproof pan on the other side of the grill. When the interior of the covered grill reaches 170 degrees, drain the wood chips and sprinkle them over the hot coals.

Put the softened butter in a bowl, add the parsley, sage, rosemary, thyme and shallots or scallions, and mix with a fork. Season with salt and pepper to taste. Stuff the herb butter evenly under the turkey skin, using the fingers of one hand to loosen the skin as you spoon the butter into the space between it and the meat.

Smoke the turkey breast on a lightly oiled grill over the pan for 3 to 3½ hours until a meat thermometer registers 150 degrees, adding additional hot coals and wood chips to the grill to maintain a temperature of 160 to 180 degrees. Let the turkey breast stand for 10 minutes before slicing. Serve hot, warm or at room temperature with the cranberry chutney.

Use an ordinary oven thermometer to gauge the temperature in the grill during smoking.

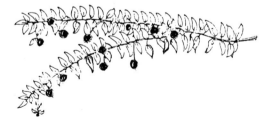

Barbecued Beef Brisket

Serves 8

Smoking a brisket of beef is an all-day affair, but by the time the last coals die, you will have one of the most delicious smoked foods we have ever tried. Plan to make this for a weekend picnic when friends and family come over for an afternoon of relaxation or a pick-up game of softball. After a day in the sun, they will happily indulge in the smoky beef sandwiches, slathering barbecue sauce on the meat with gusto. Buy the softest rolls you can find. You can join in the day's activities, too—just keep an eye on the fire to ensure the temperature is maintained.

9-pound untrimmed beef brisket
Texas Dry Rub (see page 56)
16 soft rolls
Star-Spangled Barbecue Sauce (see page 55)

Cut the brisket in half crosswise. Rub both sides with the Texas Dry Rub and let stand at room temperature for 2 hours or for at least 4 hours to overnight chilled. If chilled, let the brisket come to room temperature before smoking.

Soak a couple handfuls of wood chips in water to cover. Mesquite is best.

Build a medium fire (about 16 briquets) on the bottom of one side of the grill. Place a heatproof pan on the other side. When the interior of the covered grill reaches 200 degrees, drain the wood chips and sprinkle them over the coals.

Smoke the brisket over the pan for about 7 hours, adding additional hot coals and wood chips as necessary to maintain a temperature of 190 to 220 degrees. Slice the beef thinly across the grain. Serve on the rolls with warm Star-Spangled Barbecue Sauce on the side.

CHAPTER 6

EASY MARINADES AND SAUCES

P art of the reason foods cooked over open fires taste so good is because more often than not they have been steeped in a flavorful marinade for an hour or more, rubbed with pungent spices or liberally brushed during cooking with a saucy baste. Marinades, dry rubs and bastes, which contribute special flavor to grilled foods, also tenderize the meat and hold in juices as the food sizzles over glowing coals.

All marinades contain acid in the form of vinegar, lemon juice, wine, soy sauce and so on. While providing flavor, the acid also tenderizes tough cuts of meat—a boon to the budget-conscious griller as well as to anyone who likes the good, bold flavors of meats such as London broil and short ribs. Dry rubs, used most often in Texas and the Southwest, are mixtures of herbs, spices and (often) fiery chilies rubbed directly on the meat before grilling. Bastes are applied during cooking to add flavor and seal in juices. Marinades are frequently used as bastes (usually after being strained) and bastes sometimes serve as sauces at the table. Barbecue

53

sauces, which to most of us are spicy, sweet-sour to-mato-based concoctions, are generally served with the meat after it is cooked. Without marinades, bastes and sauces, no doubt grilled foods would lack a great deal of zesty good flavor. With them, they taste terrific.

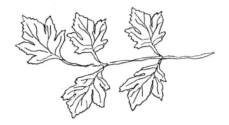

Herb Butter

Makes about ¹/₂ cup

Herb butter can be frozen, well wrapped in aluminum foil, for at least a month. It's great to have on hand to flavor grilled fish and meat or spread on warm bread; it even adds flavor to vegetable soups and stews.

Make thyme butter to top meats, such as sirloin steak (page 13) and chicken; sage butter is delicious with corn on the cob (page 40); rosemary butter is great with roasted onions (page 42), lamb and pork; tarragon butter and cilantro butter taste wonderful on fish; and oregano butter enhances grilled tomatoes (page 37) and other vegetables. Of course, you can create your own combinations with whatever fresh herbs are on hand. Use your imagination and your own good instincts.

> 8 tablespoons (4 ounces) butter, softened
> 3 tablespoons finely chopped fresh herbs, or
>   2 tablespoons finely chopped parsley and
>   1 teaspoon dried herbs
> Salt and pepper

Put the softened butter in a bowl, add the chopped herbs and mix well with a fork. Season with salt and pepper to taste.

Star-Spangled Barbecue Sauce

Makes about 2 cups

The myriad ingredients in the store-bought condiments used in this robust barbecue sauce give it a complex, full flavor—just right with beef and chicken when you want a "real" American barbecue sauce.

> *4 tablespoons (2 ounces) butter*
> *1 large onion, finely chopped*
> *2 cloves garlic, finely chopped*
> *1 cup ketchup*
> *1 cup chili sauce*
> *1/2 cup packed light brown sugar*
> *1/2 cup cider vinegar*
> *2 tablespoons steak sauce, such as A-1*
> *2 tablespoons prepared mustard*
> *2 tablespoons Worcestershire sauce*
> *Tabasco sauce*

Heat the butter in a medium-sized saucepan over moderate heat. Add the onion and garlic and cook, stirring, for about 8 minutes until the onion is soft.

Stir in the ketchup, chili sauce, brown sugar, vinegar, steak sauce, mustard and Worcestershire sauce and bring to a simmer. Decrease the heat and cook gently, stirring often, for 45 minutes until slightly thickened. Season with Tabasco to taste.

If you are using a barbecue sauce containing tomatoes and/or sugar, do not put it on the poultry or meat too soon—it will crystallize. Instead, slather it on toward the end of cooking and pass it at the table, too.

Texas Dry Rub

Makes about ⅓ cup, enough for 8 pounds of meat

Mix up a batch of this "secret ingredient" from the great State of Texas and rub it into meat before barbecuing to discover just what makes Texas barbecue so delicious. If you like a spicier blend, add more cayenne pepper.

> *2 tablespoons chili powder*
> *1 tablespoon garlic salt*
> *1 tablespoon paprika*
> *1 tablespoon pepper*
> *1 teaspoon cayenne pepper*

Mix all the ingredients together in a bowl. Rub the mixture well into desired meat, and let stand at least 2 hours at room temperature or for 8 hours or overnight chilled before cooking.

Carolina Vinegar Baste

Makes about 2 cups, enough for 4 pounds of meat

This peppery vinegar-butter baste is as effective on grilled chicken as on pork. Of course, in the Carolinas, no self-respecting cook would dream of cooking shredded pork for "barbecue" without a similar sauce. No tomato-based barbecue sauces here, please!

> *1¼ cups cider vinegar*
> *½ cup water*

8 tablespoons (4 ounces) butter
2 tablespoons lemon juice
2 cloves garlic, finely chopped
1 teaspoon crushed red pepper flakes, or more to
    taste

Combine all of the ingredients in a medium-sized saucepan over low heat and cook for 10 minutes. Cool completely. Any leftover baste can be brought to the boil and used as a side sauce for the meat.

Garlicky Lemon Marinade

Makes about 1 ²/₃ cup, enough for up to 4 pounds of meat

Anyone who likes garlic (and there are lots of us!) will appreciate this simple blend of ingredients. Use it on chicken, fish and shellfish for a good dose of the pungent bulb.

> 1 cup olive oil
> ¼ cup lemon juice
> 2 tablespoons Dijon mustard
> 3 cloves garlic, crushed
> Pepper

Do not be tempted to cut back on the oil in a marinade. It is an essential means of carrying the other flavors throughout the meat. Oil also lubricates the meat and minimizes sticking on the grill.

Combine all the ingredients in a medium-sized bowl. Marinate the chicken for up to 3 hours at room temperature or for 6 hours chilled. Marinate fish or shellfish up to 2 hours at room temperature or for 3 hours chilled. Do not overmarinate.

Provençale Marinade

Makes about 2 cups, enough to marinate up to 4 pounds of meat, fish or poultry

For a sunny Mediterranean taste, use this marinade on chicken, veal, pork, fish and shellfish. Fragrant with olive oil, lemon juice, fresh herbs and garlic, it gives food a timeless, always delicious flavor.

When purchasing dried herbs, never buy them ground, unless you have to. You will get more flavor from the whole leaf herbs, crushing them in your palm just before adding to your recipe to release their essential oils.

1 cup olive oil
1/2 cup dry white wine
2 tablespoons lemon juice
1 tablespoon finely chopped fresh rosemary or
*   1 teaspoon dried*
1 tablespoon finely chopped fresh thyme or
*   1 teaspoon dried*
1 tablespoon finely chopped fresh oregano or
*   1 teaspoon dried*
1 teaspoon fennel seed, crushed
2 teaspoons grated orange rind
1 teaspoon peppercorns
1 bay leaf, crumbled
1 clove garlic, crushed

Combine all of the ingredients in a medium-sized bowl. Marinate meat up to 3 hours at room temperature or up to 6 hours chilled. Marinate fish or shellfish for up to 2 hours at room temperature or for up to 3 hours chilled.

Teriyaki Marinade

Makes about 1½ cups, enough for about 4 pounds of meat

Hints of ginger, garlic, sherry and brown sugar combine to produce a delightful sweet-sour marinade for beef, pork and chicken.

½ cup vegetable oil
¼ cup sesame oil
¼ cup soy sauce
¼ cup dry sherry
2 tablespoons packed brown sugar
1 tablespoon chopped fresh ginger
1 medium-size scallion, chopped
1 clove garlic, crushed

Combine the vegetable and sesame oils, soy sauce, sherry, sugar, ginger, scallion and garlic until well mixed. Marinate beef, chicken or pork for at least 2 hours at room temperature and for up to 8 hours chilled. Marinate salmon or swordfish for at least 1 hour at room temperature and for up to 3 hours chilled.

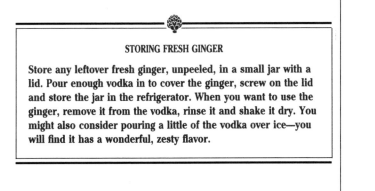

STORING FRESH GINGER

Store any leftover fresh ginger, unpeeled, in a small jar with a lid. Pour enough vodka in to cover the ginger, screw on the lid and store the jar in the refrigerator. When you want to use the ginger, remove it from the vodka, rinse it and shake it dry. You might also consider pouring a little of the vodka over ice—you will find it has a wonderful, zesty flavor.

Red Wine Marinade

Makes about 2 cups, enough for 4 pounds of meat

This hearty, robust marinade flavored with a bold blending of red wine, red wine vinegar and herbs holds up well to meats such as lamb and London broil. It is especially good with kebabs and butterflied leg of lamb. For a different taste, try it with chicken.

1 cup dry red wine
1/3 cup olive oil
1/4 cup red wine vinegar
1 small onion, sliced
2 garlic cloves, crushed
2 tablespoons chopped fresh parsley
1 tablespoon chopped fresh thyme or
   1 teaspoon dried
1 tablespoon chopped fresh rosemary or
   1 teaspoon dried
1 tablespoon chopped fresh oregano or
   1 teaspoon dried
1 teaspoon peppercorns, crushed

Combine the red wine, olive oil, vinegar, onion, garlic, parsley, thyme, rosemary, oregano and peppercorns in a bowl. Marinate meat for 2 hours at room temperature or for at least 4 hours to overnight chilled.

Avoid over-marinating food, particularly fish and shellfish, which will begin to "cook" in a marinade with a high acid content. Keep the food in the marinade as long as the recipe specifies and remember that basting during grilling adds good flavor to food, too.

Ginger Soy Butter

Makes about 1 cup

This gingery butter, bolstered by the sweet taste and unmistakable crunch of walnuts, is wonderful with grilled fish, beef or green vegetables.

8 tablespoons (4 ounces) butter, softened
4 teaspoons soy sauce
1 tablespoon finely grated fresh ginger
1 scallion, white and green part, chopped
½ cup finely chopped walnuts

Combine the butter, soy sauce, ginger and onion in the bowl of an electric mixer. Beat until fluffy. Stir in the walnuts.

Transfer the butter to a crockery or glass bowl. Cover and chill before serving. The butter keeps in the refrigerator for a week and in the freezer for up to a month.

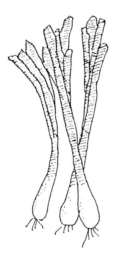

CHAPTER 7

DESSERTS FROM THE GRILL

Few of us think of using the grill to make dessert, yet nothing makes more sense. The coals are hot and ready. The rest of the meal has revolved around cooking out of doors and so it makes sense that the end should, too. While poking long sticks through marshmallows may be as far as you want to go when it comes to grilled desserts, take a look at the following recipes. All involve fruit, which we think is the best bet over charcoal, and all are very simple and quick.

Grilled fruit keeps its texture and vibrant color. Even the fruit and berries in the cobbler, baked next to hot coals for a brief half hour or so, are bright and firm. Fresh fruit, bought in season and filled with flavor, tastes wonderful after a satisfying meal, and when it is grilled, it tastes even better. It needs only to be lightly sweetened and quickly cooked over a still-hot fire as the day's light fades and dinner's conversation relaxes.

Brandied Fruit Kebabs

Serves 6

When the meal calls for nothing more elaborate for dessert than fresh fruit, yet you are in the mood for something a little special, try these buttery, brandy-scented kebabs. They couldn't be easier to assemble and take only minutes over the hot coals. Try them over vanilla ice cream—sinfully good.

> *1 small ripe pineapple, peeled, quartered*
> *and cored*
> *6 ripe plums, halved and pitted*
> *6 ripe apricots, halved and pitted*
> *4 tablespoons (2 ounces) butter*
> *3 tablespoons brandy or Cognac*
> *4 tablespoons sugar*

To pare and core a pineapple, stand it upright on the counter and use a large, sharp knife to slice off the outside skin. Quarter the peeled fruit vertically and cut out the core.

Make a medium-hot charcoal fire according to the directions on pages 8–10.

Cut each pineapple quarter into 6 chunks. Thread the pineapple, plums and apricots, alternating, on each of 6 skewers. Heat the butter in a small saucepan over moderate heat and stir in the brandy. Baste the fruit with the butter. Sprinkle the fruit with the sugar.

Cook the fruit on a lightly oiled grill over the medium-hot coals, turning and basting frequently with the melted butter, for about 6 minutes until the fruit is lightly browned. Serve immediately.

Bananas Creole

Serves 6

Reminiscent of Bananas Foster, these rich, sweet grilled bananas are so good over ice cream that you will hesitate before ever again serving plain old chocolate sauce. Wrapped in foil packets, they can be assembled before the meal and popped on the coals minutes before serving.

> *6 ripe bananas, peeled and halved crosswise*
> *6 tablespoons brown sugar*
> *6 tablespoons (3 ounces) butter, softened*
> *6 tablespoons rum*
> *2 pints vanilla ice cream*

Make a medium-hot charcoal fire according to the directions on pages 8–10.

Put 1 banana, 1 tablespoon brown sugar, 1 tablespoon butter and 1 tablespoon rum on each of 6 pieces of aluminum foil. Fold the foil up to form a packet, enclosing the ingredients. Cook the packets on a grill over the medium-hot coals, turning occasionally with tongs (do not pierce the foil), for about 5 minutes. Open the packets, pour over bowls of ice cream and serve immediately.

Grilled Cinnamon Peaches

Serves 6

When the summer's peaches are at their juicy, sweet best, try them over the grill with just a bit of cinnamon and a generous amount of butter. They are truly magnificent.

> 6 ripe peaches, halved and pitted
> 4 tablespoons (2 ounces) butter, melted
> 2 teaspoons cinnamon
> 2 pints vanilla ice cream

Make a medium-hot charcoal fire according to the directions on pages 8–10.

Baste the peaches with the melted butter. Cook the peaches on a lightly oiled grill over the medium-hot coals, cut sides down, for about 2 minutes until the peaches begin to brown. Turn the peaches, baste again, sprinkle with the cinnamon and cook for another 2 minutes until the peaches are tender. Serve immediately over bowls of vanilla ice cream.

Fruit always tastes best when bought in its season. Strawberries in June will be sweeter than any purchased in November; peaches, plums, apricots and nectarines are ripe in the summer months, as are berries such as blueberries and blackberries. Tropical fruit, such as bananas and pineapple, are very good almost all year.

Nectarine
Upside-Down Cake

Serves 6 to 8

Sweet nectarines are a pleasant change from pineapple rounds on top of a simple cake—just right for summertime entertaining, particularly since the cake can bake while you are serving the rest of the meal.

Be sure to use light brown sugar to insure the cake has the right color and texture.

TOPPING:

4 tablespoons (2 ounces) butter
3/4 cup packed light brown sugar
1/4 cup peach or apricot nectar
3 ripe medium-size nectarines or peaches, pitted and sliced

1 1/2 cups all-purpose flour
1/2 cup sugar
2 teaspoons baking powder
1/2 teaspoon ground nutmeg
1/2 teaspoon cinnamon
1/4 teaspoon salt
8 tablespoons (4 ounces) butter, melted
1/2 cup milk
1 large egg, lightly beaten

Build a hot charcoal fire on one side of the grill according to the directions on pages 8–10.

Heat 4 tablespoons of butter in a medium-sized saucepan over moderate heat. Remove the pan from the heat and stir in the brown sugar and peach nectar until smooth. Pour the mixture into the bottom of a 10-inch round cake pan. Put the nectarines on the bottom of the prepared pan in 2 concentric circles.

Stir together the flour, sugar, baking powder, nutmeg, cinnamon and salt. Make a well in the center, pour in the 8 tablespoons of melted butter, milk and egg and mix until smooth. Pour the batter over the nectarines and spread evenly with a spatula.

Bake the cake on one side of the grill next to, but not above, the hot coals, covered, for 30 to 40 minutes until a toothpick inserted in the cake comes out clean. Let the cake stand for 5 minutes. Run a knife around the inside edge of the pan, invert the cake onto a platter and serve warm.

Summertime Cobbler

Serves 6 to 8

Berries and fruit never taste as good as when they are in season in high summer. One of the best ways to enjoy them is in a juicy, warm cobbler. Toss the fruit together, add sugar and spice and cover it with a soft, sweet dough. Bake the cobbler in the grill next to banked hot coals. It takes about 30 minutes to cook so it can be baking while you are eating the rest of the meal.

8 ripe peaches, halved, pitted and cut into sixths
1 pint blueberries
1 pint blackberries
1 1/2 cups sugar
Juice and grated rind of 2 small lemons
10 tablespoons (5 ounces) butter
1 3/4 cups all-purpose flour
3 tablespoons sugar
1 tablespoon baking powder
1/2 teaspoon salt
2 3/4 cups heavy cream
4 tablespoons confectioners' sugar

If you cannot find blackberries in the markets, buy boysenberries instead. A little bigger and sometimes juicier than blackberries, they have a slightly more intense flavor.

(continued)

Make a hot charcoal fire on one side of the grill according to the directions on pages 8–10.

Lightly butter a 9-by-13-by-2-inch baking dish. Put the peaches, blueberries and blackberries in the dish. Sprinkle the fruit with the sugar, lemon juice and rind, dot with 4 tablespoons of butter and mix well.

Combine the flour, sugar, baking powder and salt in a large bowl. Add the remaining 6 tablespoons of butter and quickly cut it into the flour with a pastry blender or 2 knives until the mixture resembles coarse crumbs. Add ¾ cup of the heavy cream and stir gently until the mixture forms a soft dough. Drop the dough by large spoonfuls on top of the fruit.

Bake the cobbler on one side of the grill next to, but not above, the hot coals, covered, for 30 to 35 minutes until the topping is lightly browned.

Beat the remaining 2 cups of cream and the confectioners' sugar with an electric mixer or a wire whisk until stiff peaks form. Serve the cobbler hot or warm with the whipped cream.

A TIP TO SAVE TIME

Prepare the cobbler well ahead of time up to the point when it is assembled. Have the fruit prepared and waiting in the buttered dish, the dry ingredients for the topping set aside at room temperature and the cream measured and ready to stir in at the last minute. Simply spoon the topping on the fruit and proceed.

Grilled Pound Cake Sandwiches

Serves 6

Here's a good idea for store-bought or homemade pound cake and fresh strawberries. Toast the cake over the hot coals and then use it to sandwich the strawberries. Top the "sandwich" with sweetened whipped cream for a new twist on old-fashioned strawberry shortcake.

> *2 pints strawberries, stemmed and sliced*
> *3 tablespoons sugar*
> *1/2 cup heavy cream*
> *2 tablespoons confectioners' sugar*
> *12-ounce pound cake, cut into 12 slices*

Make a hot charcoal fire according to the directions on pages 8–10.

Toss the strawberries with the sugar, cover and chill for 2 hours.

Beat the heavy cream and the confectioners' sugar with an electric mixer or a wire whisk until stiff peaks form. Toast the pound cake over medium-hot coals, turning once, for 2 minutes until lightly browned. Make "sandwiches," using 2 toasted cake slices with the strawberries as filling. Top each cake with a dollop of the whipped cream and serve immediately.

CHAPTER 8

CONDIMENTS AND FIXINGS

Half the fun of a picnic or backyard feast is the array of condiments and fixings on the table from which everyone can pick and choose. Relishes, ketchup, mustard and herbed mayonnaise all, in their own way, turn an ordinary hamburger, grilled chicken breast or fish steak into something extraordinary. Condiments accent and highlight the food, adding bright notes of flavor, texture and color as no other part of the meal can.

In this chapter there are recipes for making your own ketchup and mustard. Neither is difficult and both taste fresher and zippier than any commercially prepared version could. Because we believe homemade mayonnaise tastes far better than store-bought, especially when it might be used to complement grilled fish, we have provided a foolproof recipe to encourage you to take the time to make your own. A couple of relishes and a chunky guacamole round out the chapter, providing an assortment of fixings guaranteed to liven up your next outdoor meal with dash and style.

Guacamole

Serves 6

Chunky guacamole turns a plain meal into a Mexican-style fiesta. Spoon some into a rustic crockery bowl and serve it with corn chips to get a backyard party off to a good start or use it as a condiment with burgers.

> *3 ripe medium-size avocados, halved, pitted and skinned*
> *¼ cup finely chopped white onion*
> *1 ripe medium-size tomato, peeled, seeded and chopped*
> *1 clove garlic, finely chopped*
> *2 tablespoons lime juice*
> *2 tablespoons chopped fresh cilantro (optional)*
> *1 tablespoon finely chopped fresh chili*
> *Salt*

Black-skinned
Haas avocados
from California
make the best
guacamole.

Mash all the ingredients together in a bowl with the back of a fork until chunky and well mixed. Season with salt to taste. Press a piece of transparent wrap directly on the surface of the guacamole and chill.

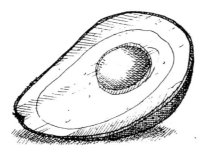

Roasted Tomato Salsa

Makes about 2 cups

Roasting the tomatoes, as they often do south of the border, gives salsa a distinctive, smoky flavor. Familiar as a dip with tortilla chips, this salsa is also a component in dishes as varied as Mexican Burgers, Fajitas and Salmon Steaks with Salsa (see pages 12, 14 and 32).

2 pounds ripe medium-size tomatoes
2 whole fresh green chilies, or more to taste
1/4 cup finely chopped white onion
1 clove garlic, finely chopped
2 tablespoons lime juice
Salt

Salsa, the Spanish word for sauce, comes in many different forms. The most common, inspired by Mexican cooking, is a chunky tomato-based cold sauce seasoned with peppers and, frequently, cilantro.

Build a hot charcoal fire according to the directions on pages 8–10.

Cook the tomatoes over the hot coals, turning often, for about 10 minutes until the skin is just charred and blackened. Cook the chilies over the hot coals, turning often, for about 5 minutes until the skin is just charred and blackened.

Put the tomatoes and chilies together in a paper bag and let them stand for about 10 minutes. Remove the skins from the tomatoes and chilies with a small sharp knife. Halve the tomatoes and squeeze gently, upside down, to remove excess seeds and moisture. Cut open the chilies and cut out the seeds and ribs. Coarsely chop the tomatoes. Finely chop the chilies. Stir together the tomatoes, chilies, onion, garlic and lime juice in a bowl. Season with salt to taste. Cover and chill for 1 hour before serving.

California
Raisin Relish

Makes about 3 cups

This robust relish is a good accompaniment to grilled pork, beef or sausages.

> *1 1/2 cups raisins*
> *16-ounce can tomatoes, with juice*
> *1/2 cup water*
> *1/3 cup white vinegar*
> *4-ounce can green chilies, chopped*
> *1/2 teaspoon red pepper flakes*
> *1/2 teaspoon salt*

Combine the raisins, tomatoes, water and vinegar in a medium-sized saucepan. Bring to the boil, lower the heat and simmer gently for 10 minutes. Stir in the chilies, pepper flakes and salt. Simmer the mixture for 5 minutes longer until the liquid has reduced so that it is at the same level in the pan as the solid ingredients.

Cool the relish and then transfer it to a glass jar or crockery bowl. Cover and chill before serving. The relish will keep for a month.

Mango Relish

Makes about 1¼ cups

There is good reason why fresh fruit relishes are popular in trendy restaurants and bistros across the country.
They taste good with everything from grilled pork
chops to swordfish and chicken breasts. Easy and quick
to make, mango relish is one of the tastiest of this style
of condiment. However, if you cannot locate fresh
mangoes, substitute a cup of finely chopped fresh pineapple or papaya.

> *1 ripe mango*
> *2 tablespoons finely chopped red onion*
> *2 tablespoons finely chopped fresh mint or*
>   *2 teaspoons dried*
> *2 tablespoons lime juice*
> *1 tablespoon finely chopped fresh green chilies*

Remove the mango pit by laying the mango, flat side
down, on a cutting surface. The pit is now horizontal
to the surface. Slice the mango about a third of the way
from the top, freeing the flesh from the pit. Turn the
mango around and slice the other side. Scoop out the
flesh from the skin with a spoon and chop it fine.

Combine the chopped mango, onion, mint, lime juice
and chilies in a bowl until well mixed. Cover and chill
for 1 hour before serving.

Vegetable Walnut Relish

Makes about 2¹/₂ cups

This colorful relish goes nicely with grilled chicken and
meat. It is easy to make if you have a food processor,
and still worth the bother of cutting up by hand if you
have no processor to entrust it to.

> *1–2 zucchini (about 8 ounces)*
> *1 large carrot, peeled*
> *1 small red onion*
> *8 radishes*
> *3 tablespoons vegetable oil*
> *3 tablespoons cider vinegar*
> *1 tablespoon Dijon mustard*
> *³/₄ cup (about 3 ounces) toasted walnut pieces*
> *¹/₄ cup packed parsley sprigs*
> *Salt and pepper*

Cut the zucchini, carrot and onion into chunks small
enough to fit through the feed tube of a food processor.
Using the medium-sized shredding disk, shred the vegetable chunks and the radishes and then transfer them
to a bowl.

Fit the processor with the metal chopping blade.
Process the oil, vinegar and mustard just to blend. Add
the walnuts and parsley and process until the walnuts
are finely chopped. Add the nut mixture to the vegetables and toss to mix thoroughly. Season with salt and
pepper to taste. Cover and chill until serving.

Homemade Ketchup

Makes about 1³/₄ cups

Homemade ketchup is more than a novelty. It tastes quite different from store-bought—better and fresher. Ripe summer tomatoes are the best kind to use when making your own, but not necessary. Use any good hothouse or hydroponic fruit, as ripe as can be, or good canned tomatoes—and enjoy having a jar of homemade ketchup in the refrigerator all year long. It keeps for about 2 weeks.

Never refrigerate tomatoes. Their flavor and composition will break down in the cold, dry environment. Instead, let off-season tomatoes ripen on the kitchen counter for a week or so until they feel slightly soft, heavier and have turned a deeper red than they were in the store.

28-ounce can crushed tomatoes or 2 pounds very
*   ripe fresh tomatoes, peeled, seeded and finely*
*   chopped*
3 tablespoons light corn syrup
3 tablespoons cider vinegar
2 tablespoons finely chopped onion
2 tablespoons sugar
1 teaspoon salt
1¹/₂ teaspoons dried sweet pepper flakes
¹/₈ teaspoon allspice
¹/₈ teaspoon ground cloves
¹/₈ teaspoon pepper
¹/₈ teaspoon celery seeds
¹/₈ teaspoon mustard seeds
¹/₂ bay leaf
1 small clove garlic, crushed

Put all the ingredients in a medium-sized, heavy-bottomed saucepan over medium-low heat. Simmer, stirring often, for 30 to 40 minutes until the mixture thickens and is reduced by half. Cool completely, cover and chill. The ketchup will improve in flavor as it ages.

Homemade Mustard

Makes about ¾ cup

As with most things homemade, once you make your own mustard you will have a hard time settling for the kind that comes in a jar. This is a crunchy, tangy mustard that tastes like a cross between fancy European mustard and ballpark yellow.

¼ cup mustard seeds
¼ cup dry mustard, preferably English
½ cup hot water
¾ cup cider vinegar
½ cup water
1 teaspoon salt
1 teaspoon turmeric
¼ teaspoon allspice
1 small onion, chopped
1 clove garlic, crushed

Stir the mustard seeds, dry mustard and hot water together in a bowl and let stand for at least 3 hours. Combine the vinegar, water, salt, turmeric, allspice, onion and garlic in a medium-sized saucepan over moderate heat. Cook for about 10 minutes until the liquid is reduced by half. Strain the liquid into the soaked mustard mixture. Scrape the mixture into a blender or food processor and process until the mustard seeds are coarsely ground.

Transfer the mustard to the top part of a double boiler set over simmering water and cook, stirring constantly, for 10 minutes until the mixture is thick but still loose. (The mustard will thicken as it cools.) Cool, cover and chill.

Homemade Mayonnaise

Makes about 1 1/2 cups

There is no mystique to making your own mayonnaise.
Simply keep whisking and take it slowly. Stir a couple
of tablespoons of chopped fresh herbs into the mayonnaise to make a pretty and elegant accompaniment to
grilled fish and shellfish.

> 3/4 cup olive oil
> 3/4 cup vegetable oil
> 2 large egg yolks, at room temperature
> 1 tablespoon lemon juice
> 1 tablespoon white vinegar
> 1 teaspoon Dijon mustard
> 1 teaspoon boiling water
> Salt
> White pepper

If mayonnaise
"breaks," put an
egg yolk and 1
teaspoon of Dijon
mustard in a
bowl. Slowly
whisk in the
mayonnaise, drop
by drop, and it
will re-emulsify.

Mix the olive and vegetable oils together.

Beat the egg yolks, lemon juice, vinegar and mustard
with an electric mixer or whisk until thick. Still beating,
add the oil, drop by drop. After you have added half of
the oil and the mayonnaise is well emulsified, you can
add the remainder a little faster. Beat in the boiling
water, and season to taste with salt and pepper.

INDEX